KAASU -MONEY SENTIMENTS

MANAGE YOUR PERSONAL FINANCE BETTER

MALLIKARJUNA SASALWAD MUDDUGALMATH

ISBN 979-888606714-9

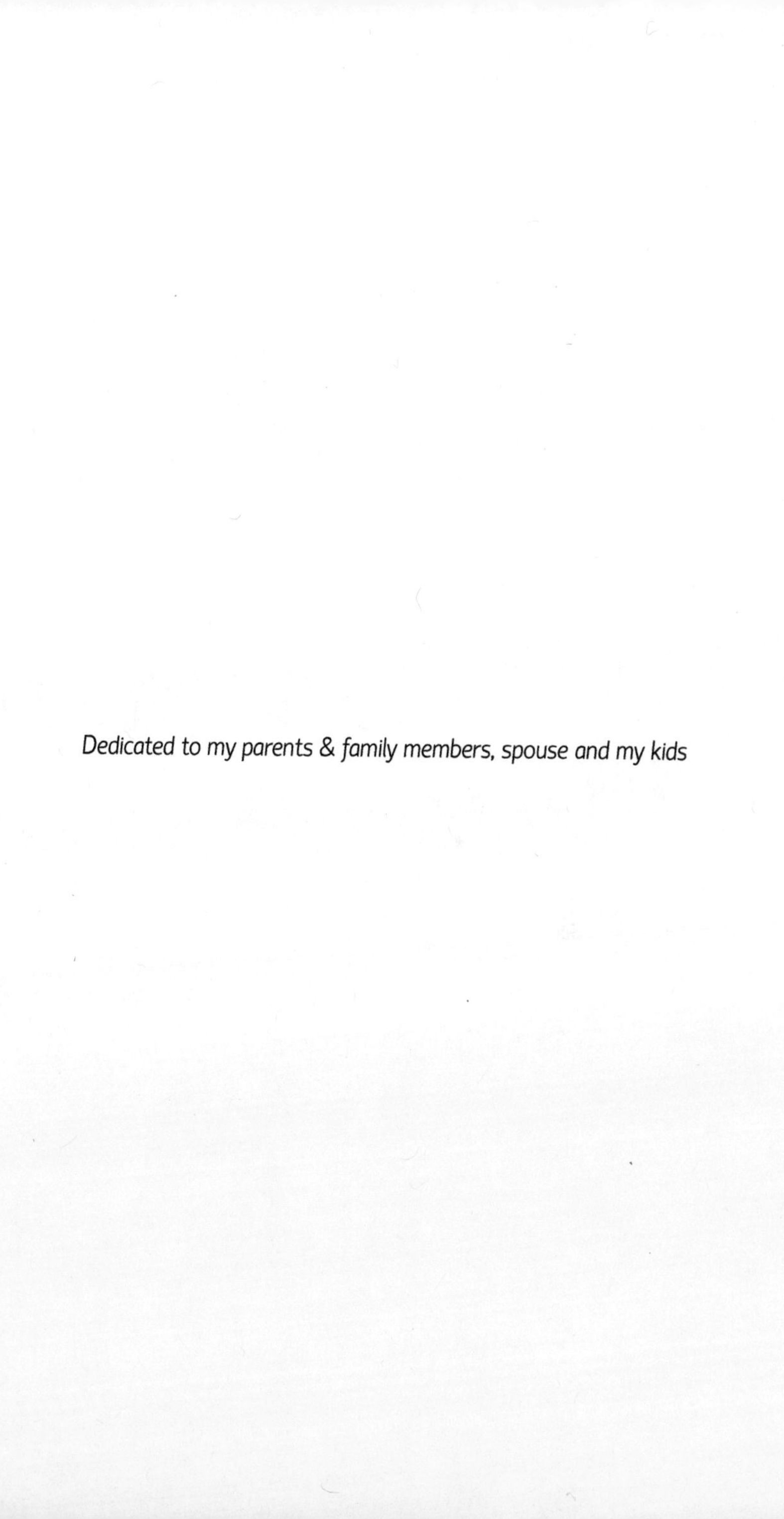

Dedicated to my parents & family members, spouse and my kids

Contents

Preface

An average person spends 90,000 hours while working but not more than 2% of the time is spent on how are spending habits, how to save, how to increase, better organize, plan, grow in financial aspects of person life.

This book is window to average person's view about how the money is treated & sentiment towards it, personal finance management by understanding basic concepts. This book will also give insight into Macro & Micro economics of country in understanding the big picture of finance.

Even though this book is written in Indian context but the core idea can be applicable to any country. Core concepts from intelligent investor, Psycology of money and One up on Wallstreet have been simplified and explained in common man terms.

Author name Mallikarjuna

Date : 22-Feb-2022

Acknowledgements

Thanks & Acknowledgements to Authors & Publishers of great books The Psychology of Money, One up on Wall Street & the intelligent investor for such a great books

Prologue

You would have greately surprised about what the title word "KAASU" mean. Kaasu in Kannada mean money or rupee. When a go street vendor or vegetable vendor , buy a KG of fruits, they will ask you for "Kaasu" which is more previelient in Bangalore I hope by now, you have got title right.

I am software professional working in TCS, Bangalore by job. Born & brought by in Davangere, Karnataka, India. In our caste & tradition, the money is not treated like a commodity but rather in the form of God/Goddess Lakshmi. The money goddess in Lakshmi, even though we are living in digital world this seems to be over exaggerated but this is true. The art & science of finding god in each and every aspect of day to day life in Indian culture.

Family the sentiments towards money from our ancestor's vs the change in viewpoint of younger generation is completely different. Including my parent earlier generations had concept on government jobs with security which most of their life is spent, survived on the single stable income source. However, as move towards fast growing the same concept exists but may not work at-least for larger population due to increase in population, shortage of jobs in public section

The idea of earning money in a family is completely discretionary but what is most important aspect about it is how it earned in legal way, taxes paid to government, ways to protect , invest, grow is different game altogether. For this to happen, you need to understand the real notion of money in real world, current trends, technology changes, true assets which bring in value proposition for you.

The notion of single earning during our parents time vs trying to have multiple sources of incomes in digital age is no more contrasting. This is the new normal as digital age is more driven by talent and not my time sitting in same position.

This book also give insights to Macroeconomics & micro economics in lay man terms for easy understanding. Also exposes you to few investing principles from great investors and authors itself. By the end of this book, you would be open your eyes towards a new world of looking at finances, I hope this will help you and your friends.

CHAPTER ONE

Inflation -Money Killer

Inflation is as violent as a mugger, as frightenting as an armed robber and as deadly as a hit man.

First of all, if you are until now not worried about Inflation, then it is time to take a minute to understand about Inflation, why it is important for every common man and what role it plays on your money. Let us take it with an example.

Let's say I am holding Rs. 100 currency today, if inflation of country is at 7% means, in next year the value of same Rs. 100 becomes Rs. 93. Ah! That is strange isn't it but have you given a thought about it anytime? If not, this is the time to think about it. Your Rs. 100 has becomes Rs. 93 without doing anything why? Because the buying cost of materials goods will increase year on year and buying capacity of money will decrease year on year.

If you hold the cash without investing it will sooner or later going to be diminished!! You cannot control the macro economics of the country but how intelligently that Rs 100 invested in safe instruments for future with least available tools or knowledge, time.

Traditionally real estate, gold, National Savings Certificate, Bonds, debt funds, Fixed deposits in our parents time used to mode of investments methods they knew and used to prefer. This seems to be true to certain extent w.r.t to gold & real estate. However the back deposits interest rates, NSC and any other secured way of investment will not going to beat inflation.

Let us assume, in current scenario banks are giving you 5% interest rate but the actual inflation itself is 7%. Which means at end of year you are losing on 2% on your actuals.

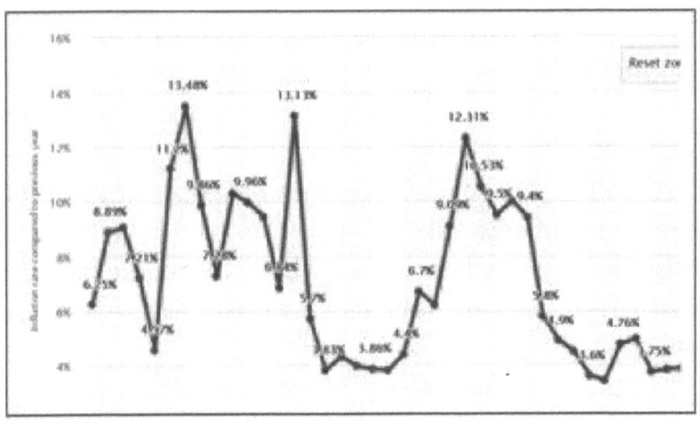

India Inflation rate

Courtesy: indiancompanies.in Figure. 1

The figure 1, shows the inflation rate in India from 1985 until now. Inflation rate as peaked during 1989 and 2007 – 2009 up to 13, 12% respectively.

Recent event when I and father had an ancestor property post selling it we had lump sum amount of money. When I asked my parents where they want to invest the money their preferred way was fixed deposits. For a normal average person, this is loss but no body will understand. Even explaining the facts of investing the money in stocks options and growth at 15 to 20 %, my parents declined as they considered it is too risky.

In my experience you should change investing principles by slowly understanding the basics of financial markets & implement them wisely by doing small experiments not by speculations or listening to any advisors. This will gives the confidence for next level of growth oppurtunity for your money and you.

CHAPTER TWO

Time & Money

Time is an illusion
- Albert Einstein

In 1990, what value we had for money is not the same now. Important point to understand is that in any asset over a period of time, slowly or steadily or drastically tend to acquire value greater than of itself. Mean time is the biggest exponential factor which adds fuel to your money.

According to the Morgan housel, biggest thing that money gets is "Time". If you have money, most of the labour jobs either physical, technical or non-technical can be get it done with no time. This concept of buying time using money is greater concept and not to be overlooked.

As a matter of fact, let us see a very few recent examples in the real world post 1990. In our home, we had the landline of BSNL which is connected over a wire. So if you had to call a person, you had to dial in number, the phone will take a while and then connects. But, getting a wired telephone connection, getting connection to your home, used to take a month or so.

So, within a very few years, when mobile phone came to India, it revolutionized the whole industry. The concept of using landline phone has vanished completely. Now a days even a very illiterate knows how to operate a mobile phone and internet. However if you look at some of telephone companies like BSNL, MTNL, over a period of time they have either become loss making business or gone out of context. So the point I am trying to bring in was, asset which was valuable become redundunt within a decade due to technology advances.

For any person on earth it is the same clock, 24 hours for everyone. But, how effectively and wisely those hours you spent and utilized, will do matter.

As the time goes values of money or so called buying power of money will decrease. Let me give an example I had personally, I had the occasion to buy a piece of land at Rs. 300 /Sq. feet with equivalent of amount of money 2006 time. However, I couldn't buy the piece of land due to another house was running we wanted to clear that as soon as possible. Unfortunately we dint buy.

Let's us a say I had bought that piece of land and left it like it, now the same piece would have costed 96,00,000 vs 72000 way back in 2006.

There is phenomenal amount of change from 72000 to 96, 00,000 with 13233 % increase. Amazing isn't it.

Similar if you had invested a new car costing 10 lacs in 2008, it would be depreciated to less than half of its value in approximately 5 years.

Age	Rate of Depreciation
0 -6 Months	5%
6months – 1 year	15%
1-2	20 %
2-3	30%
3-4	40%
4-5	50%

Depreciation Chart

From the table above its clear that 10, 00,000 would become 5 or even lesser at 5th year.

So always understand underlying asset behind the money you are putting in whether it is getting your money out of your pockets or putting money into your pocket or at-least it is growing exponentially. Invest wisely accordingly.

CHAPTER THREE

Dive In Early

When everything is moving and shifting, the only way to counteract chaos is stillness.
-Kristin Armstrong

I still remember my early days, where me and few of my frieds had a crazy behind swimming. We used to cycle around 7-8 KMs daily to get into a small canal for which river water is fed into. We wanted to dive in right early before any one comes and starts occupying the swimming area. Until the time it was 3 PM or so , we never used to go out of canal. This used to give lot of enjoyment when we were kids . The idea behind this little example, was the more early, more space we used to get.

Mr. Warren buffet started investing when he was at 10 years, he is currently net worth of $73 billion approximately 7300 crore (1 billion is 100 crores). You can't imagine or rely count warren money if it comes to you hand and will take age of lifetime to count.

Sooner or later you would realize the importance of money. The more early you realize and experience, the better it is.

Let's take an example with a SIP calculator, you do a monthly SIP of Rs, 1000 over 10 year or 120 installments. At 12% total amount of 2, 32, and 339 would be aggregated.

Getting early in game gives extra edge over time as investing horizon. Time itself is biggest exponential factor. If you set your mind, consistency is the key with time. If you combine all 3 key ingredients you will become richer than expected, slowly, steadily & consistently.

In most of traditions there is a concept called piggy bank. When any kid does some good job and to appreciate, parents will give small amount of money. The will will go ahead and store this in pot made of clay.

These pots have different shaped, sized like pig, rabbit, and elephant and once they put in money you cannot it take it back until you break it. There would be no locks on it.

The only way to open is by breaking it.

When these are full over a period of time, you will buy something valuable or most needed item. Also, this can be utilized to put back into child account.

Why do you think, I gave the above example. ? In the modern world, next generation ahead of us, gets all the facilities food, shelter without even asking. It is our responsibility to seed the idea of savings culture in our next generation before even it gets too late.

Another cultural habit you see in olden days is when a big function happens like Marriage, birth of child, baby shower, parents, family relatives give gold or money and other gifts for the occasion...These gifts will help in building a family or house at initial stages as well they will remain as valuable memories and gifts. Recent days of digital age, lot of frieds & parents also give stocks as gifts which is also left over a period of years, becomes a great gift for kids.

CHAPTER FOUR

Spending habits

"Your beliefs become your thoughts,
Your thoughts become your words,
Your words becomes your actions,
Your action become your habits"

It doesn't really matter how much you earn, if you habits of spending are not good, either sooner or later your money will get destroyed. There is proverb in Canada "If you sit & eat, put of gold is not enough" , meaning, without having good earning practices & spending habits the money will vanish in no matter of time.

Let's take an example of Ram and Sham both of them are close friend. Ram gets salary of 12, 00,000 and Sham gets 18, 00,000 annually. Ram after monthly expense invest in approximately 70, 00,000 of money in savings after 10 years at 12% interest it would have reached 8, 96,652.

However, Sham would be able to save only 20,000 because of luxury life habits and he could afford to save 12%, total amount invested turns out to be 2,56,186, Even though Sham earned 50% of salary more, but he is far below in terms of growth of money both of money they had post 10 years.

This is one of biggest culprit in our habits. You should practice savings as before start of Month or before even spending.

Spending's = Earnings - Savings but not

Savings = Earnings - Expenses

Good	Bad
Spend of most needed items	Spending on luxury , travel regular
Loans with less interest to buy assets	Personal loans, high interest rate loans, credit card default payments
Investing in appreciating assets	Investinging in depreciating assets like car, buildings
Salaried persons to save, invest before even spending on expenses at start of month	Trying to save after spending and end of month

Good habits & bad habits

CHAPTER FIVE

Savings - Biggest life saver

"Saving is gap between your ego and your income "
-Morgan Housel

In American culture, most parents will tend to give 5 to 15 % max of their total asset or earnings to next generation. However in Indian culture most of parents would probably have saved at least 70% of their total lifetime's earnings. This is major trend based on cultural values and tradition followed.

However, the world we live where lot of expected things tend to happen like accident, financial loss, job loss, market crashes, volatility etc. In 2008, when in US great depression happened, so many people lost their jobs, homes and lives. This event affected large IT companies even in India – lot of cost cutting, layoffs also happened. Most of these are driven by Macroeconomics and some are micro or even personal in nature. But, having always extra lump sum of money at hand is always gives advantage when things are not favourable in condition.

This would allow you or your family to recover quickly. Example: Let's consider Sita is running a business and suddenly due to Covid situation, her business went in loss.

She had favourable savings to support her family for 3 months without any issues. So in these 3 months, gave additional edge to recover losses or even to start a new business. This would not have possible, if there were no savings.

I still remember as a bachelor and early years when I joined Infosys, with a decent salary of approximately 3.25 lacks per annum, I used to save 50% of my earned income.

Post after, 15 years even though I though the earnings have tripled and quadruped, the savings would not reach 50%.

One of main reason for this is life style changes. The amount you spend on basics like Grocery, food, travel, phone, internet, shopping etc. As a matter of fact, both shopping “& getting food , grocery has very much digitalized thinking that it will save time but at the same time, as a human perception, you would be easily ordering on things which really don’t matter, also will make a deep hole in your pockets.

Try to keep the life style habits same without too much spending on un-necessary things. As one greater quote, if you spend on things which you don’t need, you would be soon not having money to spend of things which you need!!

CHAPTER SIX

Consistency

"It is not what we do once in a while that shapes our lives. It's what we do consistently"
-Anthony Robbins

Key ingredient in any aspect of your life either job, business, day to day life is consistency. We have to build the habit in our personal finance world as well!!

Have you realized how consistent in eating, sleeping, taking bath which are driven by physical aspects of life. Similar kind of consistency should be built in world of finance as well. Don't matter if it's Rest 100 per day or 1 lack per month, all your need is self-disciplined to able to invest.

Getting 2% profit of returns in equity makes 24% annual returns which is great. But how many of stock market traders or investors will be able to do it. Nithin Kamat founder of Zerodha explains, only 2% of traders make and above the interest yields on averge, rest of 98% will lose or loosing.

Buffet descripting investing in stock of company is like investing in underlying business. You are owning a piece of business. As long as you are able to understand that business, its cash flow, Management, growth potential over a period 7 – 10 years or more and have competitive advantage over others, you are investing a greater company.

As Suarab Mukerjee, fund manager of Marcellelus describes in one of interviews, best ways to constantly increase your wealth in share market is look for companies with clean accounting, average of greater than 15% of return on capital employed, year on year operating profits + investing is greater than zero, growth of at-least 15 – 20% consistent basis of last 10 years generally considered well.

Amy Cuddy a neuro scientist explains in her ted ex speech that, how our emotions make an impact on our body postures. If you are angry, you are breathing heavily, if you are stressed out, then you would be keeping hand on your head or neck and overall body posture would be like shrinked. Similarly, when you are happy or playing, your body posture like your shoulders will be broad, head high and arms wide open and lot of confidence.

In her research studies, she mentions how as individual we can overcome until you make it by faking it. This faking is not for someone for yourself. Just before any great event you practice assuming that same audience, bring in smile and rehearse would make you make more comfortable in actual speech itself.

Similarly, if you make a disciplined approach in your day to day activity, by making a small small changes in your consistency, behavioural habits, education to your younger ones and emotional habits then over a period of time desired goals would be achieved within a short period of time.

CHAPTER SEVEN

Compounders

"Compound interest is 8th wonder of world. He who understands it, earns it; he who doesn't, pays it"

-Albert Einstein

Einstein describes there is no 8th wonder than Compounding! Compounding works in exponential way to double the money invested in every 4-5 years. Compounded annual Growth simply called CAGR is the same which is frequently used term in stock market.

If you take an example of 1,00,000 rupees at 15% simple interest, it would take 7 years to double your money i.e. 2,00,000. However if you compound annually 5th year it would double at same rate of interest, at 10th year it would grow 4 times and 15th year 8 times and so on. Growth will be exponential. The more early you invest in compounding assists, more magic will be in future.

Similarly there is another concept called the rule of 72. This is nothing but how much years it will take you double your money. When you divide interest rate by 72 or whichever number will get you money double time.

For instance, you put in asset class which grows at 15 %

Time = 72 / 15 = 4.8 so, in 4.8 years you would have doubled your money.

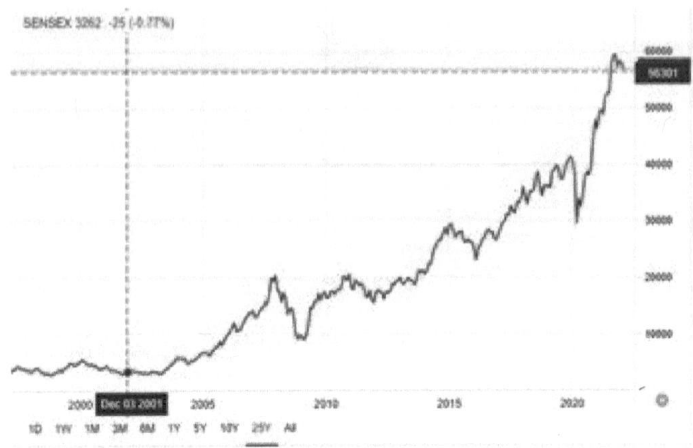

Index view

Courtesy: Tradingeconomics.com

If you look at BSE of India for last 25 year it has grown from 3500 to 60000 points on indices. 1600 times it has grown, if you had put money on just indices, it would have compounded at 1600 times to current value.

Also, one of most simplified version of putting money into stocks to get better returns in index funds. As a normal investor, sometimes it would be difficult to do fundamental analysis, technical analysis, market research on financials of the company and adjusting the strategy according to the changes in trends. As most simplified version, indexes are averages on top shares like Nifty 50 which are drivers for business. Since it is average of those companies, even a company makes profit of loss, it doesn't really matter. Most of companies including blue chips and many funds, never beat index funds or index averages consistently.

CHAPTER EIGHT

Luck

"Luck is when opportunity knocks and you answer"

Morgan Housel mentions in his book Psychology of Money 50% of the time you can be wrong and still win the race. Sometimes 80% of it you are confident winning race, still you will lose. The matter of luck plays very important aspect in life.

Let me give one real example in my real life what I had. When I was at the age of 10 years, there was a bus accident happened nearby location where approximately 100 passengers on the bus died. This happened due to the bus fell in the pond nearby. Out of these there were only 2 survivors on the incident.

There was a mid-aged man at 45, who was sitting in the bus, came out for smoking a cigarate. While smoking the cigarate within a fraction of second's bus started moving and went and fell in pond. Cigarette saved his life!! Strange isn't it. Similar, another old aged father went back due to some emergency who had on boarded the bus, but went back luckily survived.

The matter of luck plays a very significant role not only in your personal life but also in any area either in professional or business life as well.

In earlier days there used to be a game of lottery tickets which was banned in later years in India. So these games had the same concept of luck. The lottery company used to print lottery tickets in lacks. These would be sold to end customers through vendors and dealers.

Let us a say odds of winning these lottery game. Out of 1 lack tickets sold each of Rs 10, 3 ticket would be getting prizes. The odds of winning is in terms of 1 in million but the odds of losing is more predominant in these kind of games.

There is a tradition of worshipping Goddess Lakshmi if you continuously face losses in financials in Indian context. 7 Mukhi Rudraksha if you wear, there is a belief that your bad luck will be gone eventually.

There are lot of very strong support systems that are built in Indian culture to support various aspects of life. For instance post taking bath you will worship god with available resources like sacred ash called Vibuti, Sandal paste, Kumkum , flowers with sound making instruments like Shank and bell. Also, will chant mantras which has both scientific & mental health benefits over a long period of time. I truly oblige and continue to follow traditions and will also ensure that these traditions are passed to my next generation.

CHAPTER NINE

Quality & growth

"Quality is doing it right when no one is looking"
-Henry Ford

As famous Indian investor Ramdevo describes in core concepts on investing in Indian Markets, Quality, growth, longevity and Profits are main pillars when you are in investing. If your strategy built on top of these pillars, the probability of making profit over long period of time is more. Business will run either because of quality product or quality service. If there is any compromise in any then market will not value it.

In Indian context for example TCS, Infosys, Sun Pharma are few of companies which have seen as quality of business. Also, the management in these companies are very good and strong. Each of which have given consistent profit in last 10 years to investors.

Peter lynch mentions that when picking the stocks you should divide them into different categories such as how much they may tend to grow. 3-4%, 10-15%, 20-25% or cyclicals. Unless any company has growth opportunities, expansion plan, cost cutting plan, operating profits will not increase.

Longevity is how long it continue to make profits given expected profit. It is not necessary that you sit on top of 100 stocks but very few quality stocks which can get lifelong returns. Buffet made billions of money sitting on top of Coca-Cola.

Profitability in finance is core of any business out make year on year profit, reinvest profit in expansion and growth, which is benefitted for company as well as investors

No Oak tree can continue to grow till the sky, similar is the business. But, business can expand to greater scales, beyond the boundaries of any country. If you look at modern franchisees like Mc Donald's, Subway when the growth become almost maximum within US, they expanded to other countries. Now you can see the more frequent outlets even in remote parts of India.

When we have growth companies in your hand with strong MOAT means competitive advantage than others, there is no doubt that you will not make money. Looks for brands visible to you and your family members in malls, retails shops, franchise outlets, garments shops, apparels and what not.

If you come across a dominant brands expanding at very aggressive rate with a strong moat with a clean accounts, that should be one of your preferred choice to keep in your watch list.

CHAPTER TEN

Value Investing

"Price is what you pay and value is what you get "

One of best ways to avoid loss is stop listening to any so called advisors which gets with lot of news, information which actually of no use. You do your own due diligence before getting into it. There are literally 1000 of ways and techniques which no one can really understand or make profit out of it.

One of popular method used is called value investing used by Ben & Peter lynch.

PE Earnings : price you pay for getting earnings means a stock has PE of 50 and trading at 500 per share , you invest10000 bought , 500*20 = 10000 of 20 shares. You are ready to pay, 50 times its earning potential.

Let's assume EPS is 5 per share, 20 * 5 = 100 is earned in 1 year, 10000 is earned in 100 years.

Few most commonly used principles for value investing are as below:

1. Lower the PE, the better it is
2. Consistent earnings for last 5 – 10 years.
3. Strong balance sheet & low debt to equity ratio.

4. Low price to book value sometimes may not be correct

5. Insiders are buying stock or selling stock.

6. Institutional ownership – lower the better.

7. Look for discounted price, most of profit is when you buy not sell.

8. Look for cash rich companies or least debt to equity ratio which are zero chances of bankruptcy.

Value investing is not only seen in stock markets but it should be practised as a behaviour in everyday life. One of best examples of the value investing is the way our Indian women do the shopping.

I am personally not a very good fan of shopping when it comes for clothes especially. For me, main idea of shopping is to get straight the shop, look for matching shirts or pants with minimum search criteria. Maximum, I should be able to close the shopping within an hour, that's it.

In contrast, my spouse way of things in terms of same is not same. I really go along with her for shopping but if I go, I would get frustrated not because I don't want go but amount of time, she will do the search in terms of both cause & patterns. To finalize the garments, at-least 3-4 shops along with price, colour and pattern comparison with a good amount of deals. If all these are met, last is to whether to think of buying or not.

Ideally, what women are trying to do is, get the best of lots, spread across with great discounts & quality which is nothing but value investing. So is the bargain they do in vegetable market even though at very smaller level ....is that not you want at end of day?

CHAPTER ELEVEN

Job vs Business

"Pleasure in the job puts perfection in the work"
Aristotle

With my mind-set or most of Indians mind-set is idea of "Secure" job or getting so called government job. Why these notions were created is because these jobs are considered to be "Safe" and never lay-off kind of jobs.

Who don't want security? However over a period of time, the mind-set has to change or to be changed. There is nothing called Secure in this world of Choas.Let us assume, even after getting secure job, the person mets with an accident or he may fall of ill. Do you still consider that it is secure? It is just idea of secureness we have in our mind, that's it.

Most of time promptly working salaried class will be taxed by government that too before it reaches hands of common man using tax deducted at source.

Robert kiowski in Rich dad poor dad explains, how government see business and normal working class. In case of business, the government tax business post deducing all expenses. There are so many ways business can supersede taxes paid to government. I am not saying you should but government itself has given those options to you get benefitted for businesses.

Why does government do these, because the business are one's which are creating jobs, driving economy and driving force behind any country's economy. So this is the reason lot of government for example, indeed Indian tech giants like Infosys, TCS, Wipro have saved crores of rupees by paying no tax and getting even lands for free of cost from government.

As you continue to mature and grow in your financial world, you should be focussing developing business or giving jobs to lot of people and come out of your salaried zone.

This will help you in 2 ways. First, one is being salaried, you are working under someone else. Even though, you are highest level, I am sure, there would be someone on top of you. The growth here is linear, in 98% of cases.

However, when you explore the other side, there is no easy ball game but the matter of fact, you will get exposure to varied class of business, how business will grow, how they are built, once built how to expand and increase revenue. So and so forth.

Out of 10 ideas, even 1 succeeds, then this would give a tailwind to withstand the losses and make billions out of it. Similar way these, venture capitalists will work, they go and invest on many new companies, out of which even 2% succeed, and they make the billions out of it.

CHAPTER TWELVE

Alternate sources of Incomes

"Spending is quick, earning is too slow"

I am sure there are unlimited ways and opportunities in virtually any area you can think off alternate sources but I am not going to discuss many of those. However, would be discussing very few focused, tried and tested methods in this topic.

Below are few sources:

1. **Real estate**
2. **Stocks / Mutual funds / Bonds**
3. **Gold**
4. **Fixed deposits / Recurring deposits**
5. **Small business**

As you grow towards 45- 50 years of age you can take risks, change jobs, plan for better carrier, where most of time goes on consistent basis.

This is the time you should acquire wealth, create different sources of income without spending lot of time an energy. More early you do it, the biter it is. Because as you move towards older age, risk taking capacity will decrease also biggest factor is heath.

So acquiring assets income stream creation, risk taking opportunities should you finish more early better it is.

In Indian context at least, I have experienced in **Real estate** as it has lot of growth potential. As I explained few cases if you buy piece of land, it will get doubled in year or so. Why not because city is growing at that speed but buying capacity of people has increased and value of money decreased. Also, completion has increased for greedy people. You can also think of renting houses or apartments which generally considered safer at less risk but involves huge amount of capital

Another way to grow is beating inflation is through **equity markets** which is generally more risky asset class. Let's say you keep fixed deposit of 1 lack at 5% interest, inflation if at 7% ,at the end of year when it matures, you will losing 2% money.

Various techniques like buy low, sell high, purchase when market is down or simply putting money in index funds an average person can grow substantial amount of money. Also through stock splits, bones shares, dividend payments some extra income can earned.

Gold so called precious metal, we have especially women have love and affection towards it largely. At least my spouse has, every year when some lump sum amount of money is in hand, she will go and purchase gold. Gold is infect good investment.

But not as gold ornaments, where shop makes, put lot of extra like wastage charges etc. but either buy 24K gold or invest in gold bonds of RBI which gives half yearly interest. Also another problem with real gold is safety. Keeping too much in home also not good.

Fixed deposits and Recurring deposits have almost same rate of interest at 5%, if one is really not wanted to take risk, still can go for fixed deposits.

Bonds and debt funds: These are safe instruments where money is invested government schemes. Interest would less compared but better than FDS.

Small business: If you have small hobbies like a skill you can also help others by teaching and help them do it. You can start your own venture, however please ensure to start and try, test if business works before it opens to bigger audience to spend lot of money on it to avoid any losses later point in time.

CHAPTER THIRTEEN

Plan for Retirement

"Retirement is like a never ending vacation"

When you are young and energetic in life, there is nothing to worry about as long as basic needs of you and your family needs are met. Majority of people won't think about the retirement plan. When they enter into early 40- 50 years of age, by that time your earning capacity would have reduced or soon going to reduce. Planning for retirement at very early age is very important.

Another important aspect of life is Health as you move towards retirement unless you are maintaining health properly without any major illness, the spending in your olden days may also to be accounted for medical routines check-ups and ailments which will come as part growing older and older.

In India there are 2 good schemes like National Pension scheme, Atal Pension Yovanna for both organized and un-organized sector of class for better plan for retirement. Based on your contributions made until age of 60, you can get monthly pre-defined amount which would be very useful for people. Similarly 401K in US are planned for older people for retirement.

You should invest wisely and consistently so that when you become old, there is no need to worry about the finance.

It is wise to health insurance covered both for you and your spouse so that any illness and regular tests as part of old age process can take care.

Apart from the pension schemes, if you have any rental incomes from house property, farms land, and businesses built which should support your rest of retirement life without too many hurdles.

CHAPTER FOURTEEN

Margin of Safety

"Carefulness costs you nothing"

While you ride a two wheeler you wear helmet, when you drive a car you wear seat belt. All these are typical examples safety measures that is been used in an event of unforeseen circumstances. Because while you ride & drive, even though you are going in right direction or lane, someone who is drunk can come and hit you, somebody who don't can come and hit you and so on. This safety equipments or rule will save 70-80 of lives for most people. So what is similar concept when you are putting your hard earned money in any kind of financial instruments like Bonds, Stocks, Mutual funds. Benjamin Graham explains with a very beautiful concepts in his book Intelligent investor which is "Margin of safety"

Benjamin Graham describes "Margin of Safety" as the central concept of investment. He explains even before making money in stock markets, rule is not to "loose" money. How that can be achieved and foreseen is explained with beautiful concepts in next paragraph.

Let's say 10 year bonus yield is 5% and in stock made 10% of profit on your portfolio. Here you have made double the interest than bond market. You margin of safety here is 100%. Over a period of 10 years this would be 50% of aggregate in excess of stock earnings over bond.

He also mentions, if this much margin of safety is real margin of safety under favourable condition provided of minimum loss. If your portfolio is built with 20 or more stocks, probability of favourable result under normal conditions.

If similar purchases are made at average level of market over span of years, the prices paid should carry adequate margin of safety.

Probability of winning and losing with an example of American roulette example. In this wheels have 0, 00, 1...36 total of 38 slots. Casino will give maximum pay out of 35 to 1. So if you bet $1 in every number, since only 1 slot the all can drop, you would get $35 on that slot but lose $1 each of your 37 slots for net loss of $2. That $2 difference is casino's "house advantage" ensuring that on average roulette players will always loose more than they win. Both player should bet seldom as possible, casino' interest to keep roulette wheel spinning.

Likewise the intelligent investor should seek to maximize the number of holdings that offer "a better chance of profit than loss" and to widen margin of safety is by diversification.

In the roulette example, net loss of $2 is negative margin of safety. Instead it casino had rewarded with 39 to 1 the chances is 2% more winning with +2 as margin of safety. So if player bets on each number $1, every time it would be players making 2% profit.

For intelligent investor, Grahams "Margin of Safety" performs the same function. Bu refusing to pay too much for investment you minimise the chances that your wealth will ever disappear or gets destroyed.

This is very famous concept used across many financial instruments. Along with this if you spread your portfolio of stocks using diversification, it would be more safer. If any partical instrument gets, hit, balanced by the other instruments. By using these concepts in day to day, overall loss reduction ratio can be significantly reduced there by securing the wealth earned and then increasing it safely.

CHAPTER FIFTEEN

Manage personal finance

"A fool & his money are soon parted"

Most salaried class of people tend to spend the entire money they get in first 10 days of month when then get on 1st of Month. A survey report from deal sunny shows 57% of all Indians have less than 5000 in their savings account or emergency fund.

Whether you are salaried or business professional one of important aspect of personal finance is emergency fund concept. Every month move your 5% of your salary in separate account or put a half yearly amount, so that you can withstand your basic expenses without any issues.

The **emergency funds** are needed when any unplanned event happens like health issue, job loss or uncertain events. This fund will support in those cases.

Health insurance: Have at least one health insurance including your dependents to support any illness or injuries. As hospital expenses in case of surgeries it would be more, decent health insurance covering each is an added advantage.

Term insurance: If you have any large loans, please have term insurance covered up to 10 times the loan amount. Now days you can get any good term insurance at 500 per month.

Savings: As I mentioned in my earlier chapter "Spending habits", you savings should be before they are spent or start of month or any lump sum before spent on.

Plan to move at least 30-40 % of your earnings every month to another account or any of your investments planned. Maintain one account for speeding and another for savings only if possible.

Mandatory spending: Plan your spending well ahead of month like school fees, buying a house, planning for a vacation travel, etc. This includes your recurring monthly expenses like Grocery bills, water, electric, phone, internet etc. This should constitute your 30-40% overall incomes you get based on life style.

Plan for retirement: If you are not government employee, plan for the retirement schedules as I mentioned in earlier chapters. Provident fund, Atal Pension yogini, National Pension schemes are basically designed for it.

Printed by Libri Plureos GmbH in Hamburg,
Germany